Summer '99

Jamie,

I am constantly dazzled
by your brilliance!

with big love
auntie Lala

Fern Hill

A Poem by Dylan Thomas

Illustrations by Murray Kimber

RED DEER COLLEGE PRESS

Now as I was young and easy under the apple boughs
About the lilting house and happy as the grass was green,
    The night above the dingle starry,

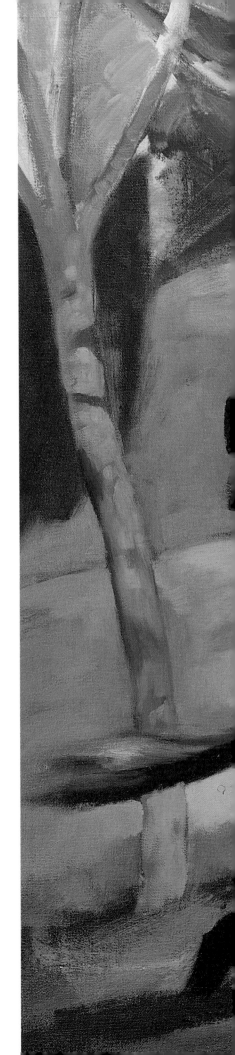

Time let me hail and climb
Golden in the heydays of his eyes,
And honoured among wagons I was prince of the apple towns
And once below a time I lordly had the trees and leaves

Trail with daisies and barley
Down the rivers of the windfall light.

And as I was green and carefree, famous among the barns

About the happy yard and singing as the farm was home,

    In the sun that is young once only,

      Time let me play and be

    Golden in the mercy of his means,

And green and golden I was huntsman and herdsman, the calves
Sang to my horn, the foxes on the hills barked clear and cold,
    And the sabbath rang slowly
    In the pebbles of the holy streams.

All the sun long it was running, it was lovely, the hay

Fields high as the house, the tunes from the chimneys, it was air

    And playing, lovely and watery

      And fire green as grass.

    And nightly under the simple stars

As I rode to sleep the owls were bearing the farm away,

All the moon long I heard, blessed among stables, the nightjars

    Flying with the ricks, and the horses

        Flashing into the dark.

And then to awake, and the farm, like a wanderer white

With the dew, come back, the cock on his shoulder: it was all

   Shining, it was Adam and maiden,

     The sky gathered again

   And the sun grew round that very day.

So it must have been after the birth of the simple light
In the first, spinning place, the spellbound horses walking warm
   Out of the whinnying green stable
      On to the fields of praise.

And honoured among foxes and pheasants by the gay house
Under the new made clouds and happy as the heart was long,
    In the sun born over and over,
        I ran my heedless ways,
        My wishes raced through the house high hay

And nothing I cared, at my sky blue trades, that time allows
In all his tuneful turning so few and such morning songs
   Before the children green and golden
     Follow him out of grace,

Nothing I cared, in the lamb white days, that time would take me
Up to the swallow thronged loft by the shadow of my hand,
  In the moon that is always rising,

Nor that riding to sleep
I should hear him fly with the high fields
And wake to the farm forever fled from the childless land.

Oh as I was young and easy in the mercy of his means,
      Time held me green and dying
   Though I sang in my chains like the sea.

Fern Hill

Now as I was young and easy under the apple boughs
About the lilting house and happy as the grass was green,
   The night above the dingle starry,
     Time let me hail and climb
   Golden in the heydays of his eyes,
And honoured among wagons I was prince of the apple towns
And once below a time I lordly had the trees and leaves
     Trail with daisies and barley
   Down the rivers of the windfall light.

And as I was green and carefree, famous among the barns
About the happy yard and singing as the farm was home,
   In the sun that is young once only,
     Time let me play and be
   Golden in the mercy of his means,
And green and golden I was huntsman and herdsman, the calves
Sang to my horn, the foxes on the hills barked clear and cold,
     And the sabbath rang slowly
   In the pebbles of the holy streams.

All the sun long it was running, it was lovely, the hay
Fields high as the house, the tunes from the chimneys, it was air
   And playing, lovely and watery
     And fire green as grass.
   And nightly under the simple stars
As I rode to sleep the owls were bearing the farm away,
All the moon long I heard, blessed among stables, the nightjars
   Flying with the ricks, and the horses
     Flashing into the dark.

And then to awake, and the farm, like a wanderer white
With the dew, come back, the cock on his shoulder: it was all
   Shining, it was Adam and maiden,
     The sky gathered again
   And the sun grew round that very day.
So it must have been after the birth of the simple light
In the first, spinning place, the spellbound horses walking warm
   Out of the whinnying green stable
     On to the fields of praise.

And honoured among foxes and pheasants by the gay house
Under the new made clouds and happy as the heart was long,
   In the sun born over and over,
     I ran my heedless ways,
   My wishes raced through the house high hay
And nothing I cared, at my sky blue trades, that time allows
In all his tuneful turning so few and such morning songs
   Before the children green and golden
     Follow him out of grace,

Nothing I cared, in the lamb white days, that time would take me
Up to the swallow thronged loft by the shadow of my hand,
   In the moon that is always rising,
     Nor that riding to sleep
   I should hear him fly with the high fields
And wake to the farm forever fled from the childless land.
Oh as I was young and easy in the mercy of his means,
     Time held me green and dying
   Though I sang in my chains like the sea.

Northern Lights Books for Children are published by
Red Deer College Press
56 Avenue & 32 Street Box 5005
Red Deer Alberta Canada T4N 5H5

Acknowledgments
Cover and text design by Kunz+Associates.
Printed and bound in Hong Kong for Red Deer College Press.

5 4 3 2 1

Financial support provided by the Alberta Foundation for the Arts, a beneficiary of the Lottery Fund of the Government of Alberta, and by the Canada Council, the Department of Canadian Heritage and Red Deer College.

COMMITTED TO THE DEVELOPMENT OF CULTURE AND THE ARTS

THE CANADA COUNCIL | LE CONSEIL DES ARTS
FOR THE ARTS | DU CANADA
SINCE 1957 | DEPUIS 1957

Canadian Cataloguing in Publication Data

Thomas, Dylan, 1914–1953.
Fern Hill

(Northern lights books for children)
A poem.
ISBN 0-88995-164-0
1. Children's poetry, Welsh. I. Kimber, Murray, 1964– II. Title. III. Series.
PR6039.H52F47 1997   j821'.912   C97-910023-2

The Artist
Murray Kimber has selected two images from this book and created a series of signed, limited edition reproductions. The run for each edition is 300 and images are available individually or as a package. The reproductions are printed on 80 lb. Quintessence dull, a high-quality archival paper and have been individually signed and numbered by the artist.

To order send cheque or money order to:
Fern Hill Prints
C/o Drawn and Quartered Inc.
1900 C 11th Street SE
Calgary, AB T2G 2G2 Canada
Phone (403) 264 1541
When ordering please indicate the reproduction of choice and make cheque payable to Drawn and Quartered, Inc. All prices in Canadian currency. Prices include applicable Canadian taxes and shipping within Canada and the USA. Foreign orders add CDN $7 for shipping. Please allow four weeks for delivery.

That Time Would Take Me
Paper size: 24 x 23 inches
Image size: 20 x 19 inches
Price: CDN $85

So Few Morning Songs
Paper size: 18.5 x 24 inches
Image size: 14.5 x 20 inches
Price: CDN $75

Order both reproductions for CDN $145